TEN COMMON SENSE STEPS
ON YOUR WAY
TO SUCCESS

" A Sensible Approach To Living Life"

WORKBOOK

Henry O. Adkins

Fifth printing Summer Edition 2017
Fourth printing Summer Edition 2014
Third printing Spring Edition 2013
ISBN 0-9672605-0-7

Foreword

Every effort has been made to produce a workbook that covers the subject of the workshop that is informative and factual. Information was researched and gathered from Newspaper, periodicals and the internet. All researched sources are cited throughout the workbook.

Privacy Notice

The material contained in this Workshop workbook is solely intended for the individual and private use of the participants of the workshop. Prohibited use includes but is not limited to the copying, renting, leasing, selling, distributing, transmitting or transfer of all or any portions of the material, or use for any other commercial and/or solicitation purposes of any type without the expressed written permission from the Author and Publisher.

Preface

I believe in the power of Common Sense. Common Sense is valuable in all situations. There are Common Sense ways of doing everything in your everyday life. Having and following a Common Sense Guide is important and necessary for a fulfilling life. That guide within can be tapped into and used at any time. What is needed has been with you from the beginning. That Common Sense guide is the Bible. Robert E. Criner, a national motivational speaker, says, "Everything that I teach about personal growth and development, I take from the Bible. Everything needed for your moral stability and to motivate the spirit is found in the Bible." He delivers this message in a clear uncomplicated down home way. That is the approach offered here. It gives the means for dealing with the barriers and difficulties of everyday life. I know that I am successful and that I am blessed. I do not have a lot of money, but I am rich. I do not have a top executive position, but I have status with God.

Common Sense has helped me to recognize that I have a great life, and for that, I am grateful. By following the steps in this workbook and applying them, you will see how successful you already are and use that realization to build a prosperous life and career.

"Breaking out of the Paper Sack"

Do you know someone who is a genius? Does that person know something about everything? Is he a trivia pursuit expert? Can he fix anything that is broken, but seems to lack common sense. My grandmother would say this about such a person; "that boy can't common sense his way out of a paper sack." Another of her frequent quotes was; " that person aint got the common sense God gave a doodle bug." She was direct and always 'right on the money' with her opinions of people. There may be times when all of us feel like we're trapped in a paper sack, but with a little bit of common sense we can fight our way out. So many of us do not apply the common sense that God has given us, and we keep ourselves trapped in that paper sack.

Contents

NOTE TO SELF...

For the love of stuff (money) is the root of all evil.

I Timothy 6-6

STEP ONE

Recognize Success

"Recognize the extraordinary in the ordinary"

How will I know it when I see it? Many people don't believe they are successful unless they can display some tangible big time stuff, like a new luxury automobile, a big house, fine clothes or a large bank account. All these things are just stuff. Stuff does not always equal success. True success is not to be measured by the amount of stuff you acquire. There are many so-called successful people who work long hours every week just to acquire stuff. Some turn to drugs or become addicted to their work. They work hard and long to increase their bank accounts so they can buy more stuff. Either of these addictions will cause you to eventually lose earning power and all of your accumulated "stuff." "Stuff" to many people is success, but it is not. You need to change. It's just stuff! Somehow, someday you will recognize real success. We are all good at something, but sometimes we don't recognize our successes. We are blinded by what the world says success is … ie… cars, big houses, money, partying and more. Don't be afraid make a change in your life. You deserve Real Success. You need not look very far. It is within you. Everything you need for Success has been with you since birth. God has not given you the spirit of Fear, but rather the ability to recognize your gift of Success. So, don't hesitate make that CHANGE and know your **life's purpose**.

Read these excellent books on developing life purpose and intentions.

1. Eckhart Tolle's *A New Earth: Awakening to Your Life's Purpose*
2. Dr. Wayne Dyer's *The Power of Intention*

Make a list of all your activities, professionally, socially, etc...and there you will make a change and find your true successes.

Recognizing Success

Professionally_____

Socially_____

Family _____

Employment_____

Common Sense for Life/Recognize Success
"Trust God, have faith in him, know who you are and know whose you are."

1. Recognize that your thoughts will determine your success.

For as he thinks in his heart, so is he ...Proverbs 23:7

2. Recognize that you have strengths and abilities.

But David said to Saul, "Your servant has been keeping his father's sheep. When a lion or a bear came and carried off a sheep from the flock, I went after it, struck it and rescued the sheep from its mouth. When it turned on me, I seized it by its hair, struck it and killed it. Your servant has killed both the lion and the bear; this uncircumcised Philistine will be like one of them, because he has defied the armies of the living God. The LORD who rescued me from the paw of the lion and the paw of the bear will rescue me from the hand of this Philistine." Saul said to David, "Go, and the LORD be with you." ...1 Samuel 17:34-37

3. Recognize that God is there to protect you.

Then Nebuchadnezzar said, "Praise be to the God of Shadrach, Meshach and Abednego, who has sent his angel and rescued his servants! They trusted in him and defied the king's command and were willing to give up their lives rather than serve or worship any god except their own God. ...Daniel 3:28

4. Recognize that laws or decrees cannot keep you from God.

The royal administrators, prefects, satraps, advisers and governor save all agreed that the king should issue an edict and enforce the decree that anyone who prays to any god or human being during the next thirty days, except to you, Your Majesty, shall be thrown into the lions' den. Now, Your Majesty, issue the decree and put it in writing so that it cannot be altered—in accordance with the law of the Medes and Persians, which cannot be repealed." So King Darius put the decree in writing. ...Daniel 6:7-9

5. Recognize that you can do all things through Christ.

I can do all this through him who gives me strength. ...Philippians 4:13

What Is Success To You? How does money, wealth and stuff figure into your definition of success?

_____

_____

_____

_____

Can you personally consider yourself successful without money and stuff? Without your dream job?

_____

_____

_____

_____

Why is money and stuff so important to many of us? And not so much to others?

_____

_____

_____

What are the gifts of success that you have?

_____

_____

_____

_____

_____

_____

_____

_____

_____

_____

_____

What are you doing to improve your gifts?

_____

_____

_____

_____

_____

_____

_____

_____

_____

_____

Choose Success
"Don't let fear limit your success"

Being afraid, and being scared, will cripple you. It stops growth. Without growth, success stalls. Fear as we know it, as it has been taught to us, gives us an excuse not to do a lot of things; not to strive toward the goals for success. We must change our thinking about fear. We know that fear is negative, but you can turn that fear around and make it a positive tool. Never let fear stop you from reaching your goal, but rather use fear to elevate you and your goals. Make fear a positive tool. For our purposes "Fear" is an acronym for Face the situation head on. Evaluate the situation. Analyze your position. React accordingly. Face situations by not running from or avoiding them. Stand up to your adversities. Don't let anything or anybody scare you away from the things that will help you reach your goals.

NOTE TO SELF...

When you start large, and spend little or no time building a sound foundation, a fall is eminent. Remember Humpty Dumpty?!

Henry O from Plano

STEP TWO

Start Small
"Accept the little successes and prepare yourself for the big ones"

Most people do not recognize themselves as successful unless they are at the highest level of their career or profession. Many want to start at the top but do not want to do the work to get there. They do not believe it is necessary. Some believe there is a quick path to success and that taking short cuts is O.K. They are certain that is how others landed their on top. That is seldom or never the case. They are wrong. There may be some people who get to the top without doing the necessary work, but those who do often find themselves unprepared, overwhelmed, and lacking the skills for the tasks ahead and remaining where they find themselves. When the work is not done, what was thought to be a dream can become a night mare. You must start small with humility and do the work whatever it is to the best of your ability.

Make a list of your long and short term goals. List the steps you will take to reach your goals.

Goal Setting Suggestions

1. Make goals reachable by taking small easy steps.

2. Make your timeline one that is not too short or too far away.

17

3. If you have to re-set your timeline do it sooner rather than later.

4. If you have to change your goal that's ok, just remember to always have goals.

5. Write down your goals and if need be re-write them again.

6. When you reach a goal make another.

7. Start small and do the work.

Common Sense for Life/Start Small

To reach major goals it takes time. It is a long journey, but "a 1000 mile journey begins with the first step". Think BIG but **start small.**

1. Don't get in a hurry for wealth. Take your time and let things develop.

*A faithful man will abound with blessings, but whoever hastens to be rich **will not go unpunished.*** *Proverbs 28:20 ESV*

"I am come that they you have life, and that you might have it more abundantly." John 10:10 KJV

2. Don't fall in love with money because money comes and goes.

   *Keep your life free from love of money, and be content with what you have, for he has said, "I will never leave you nor **forsake** you." Hebrews 13:5*

3. Start small but think big. Put God in your life and things will come to you.

   *Not that I am speaking of being in need, for I have learned in whatever situation I am to be **content**. Philippians 4:11 ESV*
   *Now there is **great gain** in godliness with **contentment**, 1 Timothy 6:6*

   *But seek first the kingdom of God and his righteousness, and all these things will be **added** to you. Matthew 6:33 ESV*

4. To start small does not mean to stay small, but rather take your time and grow the right way.

   *Better is a little with righteousness than great revenues with **injustice**. Proverbs 16:8 ESV*

   *Better is the little that the righteous has than the abundance of many **wicked**. Psalm 37:16 ESV*

   *Better is a poor man who walks in his integrity than a rich man who is **crooked** in his ways. Proverbs 28:6 ESV*

5. Your Success is controlled by the image **YOU** have for yourself

   For as a man thinks in his heart, so [is] he... Proverbs 23:7

   A person is limited only by the thoughts that he chooses. — James Allen

NOTE TO SELF...

Fear less, hope more. Whine less, breathe more. Talk less, say more. Hate less, love more. Good things can be yours. …Anonymous

STEP THREE

Keep It Simple Sigmond (KISS)

"To Complicate Is To Frustrate" …Henry O. Adkins

Using common sense to parent your children will bring them closer to you. Using common sense in your marriage, makes it stronger. When you use common sense on the job, you suffer less stress, receive more promotions and enjoy the job more. When common sense is applied to your life you are happier, you laugh more and live longer. When you apply common sense it makes your life simpler. It offers a reasonable way of doing things. Many refer to this as the KISS method, "Keep It Simple Sigmond." Using KISS will keep you grounded.

How to Keep It Simple

1. Having a lot of Material Things will not bring Happiness. Having what you need might.

2. Think before you buy. Ask yourself do I really need this?

3. Save a little of your income, for a rainy day is sure to come.

4. Know what you want in life and make a plan.

5. Give away or throw out all unneeded stuff. If you haven't use it in a year it's time for it to go.

6. Live below your means.

7. Be of service to others.

8. Spend more time at home with your spouse and family.

9. On Some days do absolutely nothing. Just relax.

Common Sense for Life/"Keeping It Simple"
"To Complicate Is To Frustrate" ...Henry O. Adkins

1. **Love the Lord** your God with all your heart and with all your soul and with your mind and with all your strength. *Mark 12:30(NIV)*

2. The second is this: **Love your neighbor** as yourself. There is no commandment greater than these. *Mark 12:31(NIV)*

3. "If you love me, you will **obey what I command**. *John 14:15(NIV)*

4. So in everything, **do to others what you would have them do to you,** for this sums up the Law and the Prophets. *Matt. 7:12(NIV)*

5. **Give**, **and it will be given to you**. A good measure, pressed down, shaken together and running over, will be poured into your lap. For with the measure you use, it will be measured to you." *Luke 6:38(NIV)*

6. **Trust in the LORD** with all your heart and lean not on your own understanding; *Proverbs 3:5 (NIV)*

7. Then Peter came to Jesus and asked, "Lord, how many times shall I **forgive my brother or sister** who sins against me? Up to seven times?" Jesus answered, "I tell you, not seven times, but seventy-seven times. *Matthew 18:21-22(NIV)*

Take a look at your life and make a list of ways to **simplify it**.

At work_____

_____

_____

_____

At play_____

_____

_____

_____

At home_____

_____

_____

_____

_____

_____

NOTE TO SELF…

Choose Joy and you will have Joy. "I choose Joy."

Henry O from Plano

STEP FOUR

Expect the Best From People

"People may give up on you, but never give up on people"

Common sense helps you understand that, to get the best, you must expect the best and you must give the best to receive the best. The best people are happy people choose joy.

Common Sense for Life/"Choose Joy"
*May the God of hope fill you with all **Joy** and peace ...Romans 15:13*

1. Joy does not depend on What You Have!
   Not that I speak from want; for I have learned to be content in whatever circumstances I am. I know how to get along with humble means, and I also know how to live in prosperity; in any and every circumstance I have learned the secret of being filled and going hungry, both of having abundance and suffering need. ...Philippians 4:11-12

2. Our JOY is In The Lord
   The LORD is my strength and my shield; my heart trusts in him, and I am helped. My heart leaps for joy and I will give thanks to him in song...Psalm 28:7

3. True JOY Is Being In The Presence Of The Lord
   You make known to me the path of life; you will fill me with joy in your presence, with eternal pleasures at your right hand... Ps 16:11

4. Count It All JOY
   My brethren count it all joy when ye fall into divers temptations; Js 1:2

5. When times are tough there is still JOY in Christ Jesus. Tough times don't last, TOUGH PEOPLE DO!
   weeping may endure for a night, but joy comes in the morning. Psalm 30:5

To expect the best from people, you must develop the right **Attitude**. Do not automatically expect the negative. In all situations look for the positive and stay positive within yourself. Be the example of Positivity.

1. When you change your **attitude** from negative to positive, you change your life. …*Henry O from Plano*

2. The thought (attitude) manifests as the word. The word manifests as the deed. The deed develops into habit. And the habit hardens into character. …*Buddha*

3. If you correct your mind (attitude), the rest of your life will fall into place. …*Lao-Tzo*

4. Happiness mainly comes from our own attitude, rather than from external factors. …*The Dalai Lama*

5. Excellence is not a skill. It is an attitude. …*Ralph Marston*

A change can only be done by changing your attitude. The world as we have created it is a process of our thinking (attitude). It cannot be changed without changing our thinking (attitude). ...*Albert Einstein*

We are the change we have been waiting for. ...*President Barack Obama*

What Attitude changes can you make in your life to expect the best?

1. _____

2. _____

3. _____

4. _____

5. _____

6. _____

7. _____

8. _____

_____

_____

A change of Attitude will insure your success, but you first must understand what success is and what it means to you. **Only you**.

1. Try not to become a person of success. Rather become a person of value. ...*Albert Einstein*

2. Success is not final, failure is not fatal: it is the courage to continue that counts. ... *Winston Churchill*

3. I'm a success today because I had a friend who believed in me and I didn't have the heart to let him down. ...*Abraham Lincoln*

4. Our greatest fear should not be of failure but of succeeding at things in life that don't really matter. ...*Frances Chan*

What does success mean to you?

1. _____

2. _____

3. _____

4. _____

5. _____

6. _____

7. _____

8. _____

The Only Thing To Do

Do not allow anyone to decide your life and career. That's your job. You must move forward. Moving forward is **the only thing to do**. Doing a job better than it has ever been done before is **the only thing to do**. Work to create a positive environment and atmosphere around you is **the only thing to do**. Encourage and help others around you is **the only thing to do**. Be grateful for what you have, and don't complain about what you do not have, that's **the only thing to do**. Trust that if you do what you know to be right and good, good things will come to you because, **It's the only thing to do.**

NOTE TO SELF…

If you are pushed to choose between your family or your job, choose your family.

Henry O. Adkins

STEP FIVE

Put Family First, Your Job Second

Your family is the most important part of your existence. Not your job. Not your career, but rather **YOUR FAMILY**. Always, always put your family first. If the job is a threat to the well being of your family, get another job. Picking might be slim but you can get another one. Your main job is to protect your family. That is your duty and God given responsibility. It does not mean that you should neglect your employment. You should always give your best in the workplace. But, remember do not choose your job over your family if you have to, you can always get another J. O. B.

Make a list of ways you can put your family first.

1. _____

2. _____

3. _____

4. _____

What would you do in the following situations?

1. Work overtime or attend your child's music recital.

_____

_____

_____

_____

2. Attend your child's college graduation when your boss denied you vacation time or miss the graduation stay and work to so not to put your job in jeopardy?

_____

_____

_____

_____

3. You get a call from your spouse telling you there is an emergency at home and you should come home as quickly as possible. Your boss says you can't leave after all there is an important meeting scheduled and he needs you at the meeting.

_____

_____

_____

You Can Get another Job

Your family is important. Not a job. Not a career. The family. Always, always put family first. If the job is a threat to the well being of your family, get another job. Protect your family. That is your duty. It does not mean that you neglect your job or other people. But you can get another job. There may be some good people on a horrible job. Don't give up on those people or break ties with them. You should keep a good relationship with good people, even if you leave the job. Don't ever give up good relationships with good people. *Put your family first and never give up on people.*

NOTE TO SELF…

Giving up can cause you to miss your appointment with success. Success is available. Don't give up.

…Henry O. Adkins

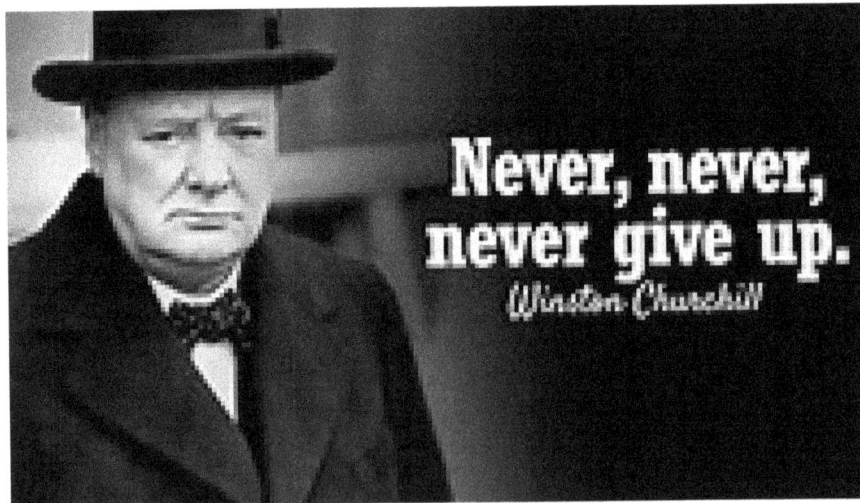

STEP SIX

A Disappointment is an Appointment with Success

Never look back. Always look forward. Look for your bright future, and know that **a disappointment is an appointment with success. Take it.** Let disappointments go. It may be hard, but the day after a disappointment, decide to put it in the past. It should not remain in your present or move to your future. Leave disappointments in the past and let them go. It is old baggage. Let it go. Get rid of it. Make room so you can take advantage of the new stuff. Turn your disappointments into re-appointments for success. Decide to make the most of each day. You can do it if you free yourself of yesterday's anger and resentments. Stop whining about what should have been or what could have been. It is important to stop blaming other people because of your disappointments. Hurt will not go away in an instant, but it is manageable. Dry your eyes and stop crying. When you do you are able to see the success possibilities available to you. Never focus on disappointments. Doing so traps you in the past and delays your future. Change your attitude and move forward. A positive attitude can help to brighten your future and make success possible. Don't get trapped in the past. Let past disappointments go. Know your past, but do not linger there. Look to the future. The best is yet to come. ***Don't let a disappointment stall your common sense to succeed.***

A disappointment can be the beginning of your Success. A disappointment is an opportunity to go from a short comer to an over comer.

Turn That Disappointment into An Appointment With Success

You have suffered a big disappointment. That hurt can be hard to bear. Although your feelings are bruised and your spirit damaged, you must not let that disappointment and hurt stop your success. Don't dwell on the disappointment. If you do it will defeat you. One or two disappointments does not spell defeat. What you must do is, Use Common Sense and turn that Disappointment into an Appointment with Success.

Common Sense for Life/Overcoming Disappointment
"Disappointments are inevitable but misery is optional"

1. Disappointments can bring hard times, but these times are not to stay, they are just passing. Let them go.

   *...And we know that **all things work together for good** to them that love God, to them who are the called according to [his] purpose. Rom 8:28*

2. Don't be disappointed because you wanted something now, things rarely happen when you think they should.

   *...Be careful for nothing; but in everything by prayer and supplication with thanksgiving let your **requests** be made known unto **God**. Phi 4:6-7*

3. You may be disappointed because a man did not like your work. Remember, whatever you do or whatever the job, do it for God and not to satisfy men.

   *...And whatsoever ye do, **do [it] heartily, as to the Lord**, and not unto men; Colossians 3:23-25*

4. Disappointments are coming but know that God blesses all good work dedicated to him and know that your help comes from him.

   *...I will lift up mine eyes unto the hills, from whence cometh my **help**. Psalms 121:1-8*

5. Don't let disappointments hold you back. Live with expectancy. Expect a great day. Expect a blessing from the Lord. Expect the best.

   *For I know the thoughts that I think toward you, saith the LORD, thoughts of peace, and not of evil, to give you an **expected end**. Jere 29:11*

6. In times of disappointment don't go it alone, know that there is strength in God.

   *... **God** [is] our refuge and **strength**, a very present help **in (times of) trouble**. Psalms 46:1-11*

7. When the fall of disappointment comes don't worry, know that the Lord is there to catch his children.

   *... Are not two sparrows sold for a farthing? and one of them **shall not fall** on the ground **without your Father**. Matthew 10:29-31*

NOTE TO SELF…

Rally in that quiet place of reflection, meditation and prayer. It is there that you can hear GOD.

Henry O from Plano

STEP SEVEN

Be Quiet and Reflect

To determine what you should do, you must first rally beneath a flag. Rally your thoughts. Find a quiet place to be with your inner thoughts. Don't talk, just think. Allow yourself to experience the phenomena of quiet while you gather your inner thoughts. Give yourself the opportunity to stand beneath your flag, whatever that flag might be. Come to a place of contentment and relaxation. That is when your mind becomes clearer. Establish your rallying place. We are bombarded with noise day and night, seven days a week. And we have accepted it as the norm. We seldom challenge it and most us are resigned to it. To rally beneath your flag you must challenge the noise and not accept it as the norm. Find that quiet place of reflection, meditation and prayer. Think on things that will not only benefit you, but others. What we give, we get. What goes around, comes around. What we send out to others comes back to us. These are universal principles. Our lives change fast. The amount of noise and stress continues to grow. A quiet rallying place is needed more today than at any other time in our lives. Take the opportunity. Rally beneath your flag. Take time to think, reflect and pray. Do this, and the answers to your questions will come. Solutions to problems will be realized.

Benefits of taking a regular Quiet time to Reflect

1. Easier to remove bad habits

2. Increased job satisfaction

3. Increased Productivity

4. Improved relations at home & at work

5. Helps ignore petty issues

6. Increased ability to solve complex problems

7. react more quickly and more effectively to stressful events

8. Develop will power

9. improved on the job relationships

Common Sense for Life/Be Quiet and Reflect

Find a quiet place of reflection and prayer. It is there you hear GOD. ... Henry O. Adkins

"Be still, and know that I am God. I will be exalted among the nations, I will be exalted in the earth!" ... Psalm 46:10*

1. When you have problems find a quiet place. Don't talk, just listen.

    *The Lord will fight for you, and you have only to **be silent**." ... Exodus 14:14*

2. Don't be in a hurry. Wait on the Lord and good things will happen.

    Be still *before the Lord and **wait patiently** for him; fret not yourself over the one who prospers in his way, over the man who carries out evil devices! ... Psalm 37:7*

    *For God alone, O my soul, **wait in silence**, for my hope is from him. ... Psalm 62:5*

    *... The Lord is good to those **who wait for him**, to the soul who seeks him. It is good that one should **wait quietly** for the salvation of the Lord. ...Lamentations 3:24-26*

3. In all situations stay calm and listen for a word from the Lord.

    *But I have **calmed and quieted my soul**, like a weaned child with its mother; like a weaned child is my soul within me. ... Psalm 13:1-2*

    *"Teach me, and **I will be silent**; make me understand how I have gone astray. ... Job 6:24*

4. Be Quiet and hear God, he is our strength.

    *For thus said the Lord God, the Holy One of Israel, "In returning and rest you shall be saved; **in quietness and in trust** shall be your strength." ... Isaiah 30:15*

Be Quiet and Listen

Listening is better than talking. When you listen and hear, you learn. Learning is how we grow. Learning is how we develop common sense; and common sense is a key element of success. The Bible states that fear of the Lord is the beginning of knowledge (common sense) listen to "wise counsel." That is real common sense. To gain common sense and understanding you must listen. There are people around you who speak great words of wisdom and do wonderful things. To learn from those people, you must listen. Listen and hear in order to learn. When you don't listen or hear, you can fall into unsavory, unflattering, even dangerous situations that could have been avoided by listening and using common sense.

Are you taking quiet time for reflection and thought?

When?_____

How many days of the week?_____

Where?_____

Is it noise proof?_____

Do you meditate, pray or just think?_____

Is it helpful?_____

If you are not, why not?_____

Do you think it could be helpful?_____

NOTE TO SELF…

The more I read about the lives of great men, the more Common Sense I acquire.

Henry O from Plano

STEP EIGHT

Common Sense, Necessary Step – Take A Risk!

Do everything in your power, with God's help, to make your family better and stronger. Train your children in the way that God would have you do. Use Common Sense by listening to others. Read, study, observe, and listen to your spouse and your inner self. Using Common Sense in family matters is a big step. It is a necessary and essential. Make sure that all your steps are guided by the Lord.

List ways to improve your life by using Common Sense.

1._____

2._____

3._____

4._____

5._____

6._____

Common Sense for Life / The Necessary Step – Take a Risk
"Playing it safe keeps you where you are. STUCK!"

1. Take a Risk. Don't wait for the best time to do something good. Whenever you do something good is always the best time. Sow a seed and enjoy the harvest.

   He that observes the wind shall not sow; and he that regards the clouds shall not reap. Ecclesiastes 11:4-6

2. Take a Risk. Give yourself away, for what you give will come back to you.

   Cast thy bread upon the waters: for thou shall find it after many days. Ecclesiastes 11:1-3

3. Take a Risk. Go somewhere you have never been before.

   For [the kingdom of heaven is] as a man travelling into a far country, [who] called his own servants, and delivered unto them his goods. Matthew 25:14-30

4. Take a Risk. Expand what you have or lose it all.

   *For unto everyone that hath **shall be given**, and he shall have abundance: but from him that hath not **shall be taken away** even that which he hath. Matthew 25:29*

5. Take a Risk. Do something. Make a decision. Get off the fence.

   If we say, we will enter into the city, then the famine [is] in the city, and we shall die there: and if we sit still here, we die also. Now therefore come, and let us fall unto the host of the Syrians: if they save us alive, we shall live; and if they kill us, we shall but die. 2 Kings 7:4

Common Sense Quotes

1. Common Sense is not so Common. ...*Voltaire*

2. It is a thousand times better to have common sense without education than to have education without common sense. ...*Robert G. Ingersoll*

3. The three great essentials to achieve anything worthwhile are, first, hard work; second, stick-to-itiveness; third, common sense. ...*Thomas Edison*

4. Common sense is the knack of seeing things as they are, and doing things as they ought to be done. ...*Harriet Beecher Stowe*

5. I always try to believe the best of everybody -- it saves so much trouble. ...*Rudyard Kipling*

6. Common sense is strengthened by joy. ...*Rebbe Nachman of Breslov*

7. The philosophy of one century is the common sense of the next. ...*Henry Ward Beecher*

8. "Don't be afraid of being scared. To be afraid is a sign of common sense. Only complete idiots are not afraid of anything." ... *Carlos Ruiz Zafón*

NOTE TO SELF…

Talk a lot, miss a lot. Listen a lot, learn a lot.
                                             …Odis Adkins

STEP NINE

Listen, Hear and Learn

The book of Proverbs is King Solomon's book of common sense. This book was written over 2000 years ago. The common sense in that book is still applicable today. King Solomon said that "a wise man will hear and will increase in learning; and that a man of understanding shall attain unto" or listen to "wise counsel." This is a lesson in real common sense. To gain common sense and understanding you must listen.

The Sayings of some Great people

1. "In this life you've got to hope for the best, prepare for the worst and take whatever God sends." ... *L.M. Montgomery*

2. "It has been my observation that most people get ahead during the time that others waste" ...*Henry Ford*

3. "Success isn't permanent, and failure isn't fatal." ...*Mike Ditka*

Make a list of sayings by great people and determine how those sayings have or can influence your life.

1._____

_____

2._____

_____

3._____

_____

4._____

_____

5._____

_____

6._____

_____

_____

Dare to Be
by
Steve Maraboli,

When a new day begins, dare to smile gratefully.

When there is darkness, dare to be the first to shine a light.

When there is injustice, dare to be the first to condemn it.

When something seems difficult, dare to do it anyway.

When life seems to beat you down, dare to fight back.

When there seems to be no hope, dare to find some.

When you're feeling tired, dare to keep going.

When times are tough, dare to be tougher.

When love hurts you, dare to love again.

When someone is hurting, dare to help them heal.

When another is lost, dare to help them find the way.

When a friend falls, dare to be the first to extend a hand.

When you cross paths with another, dare to make them smile.

When you feel great, dare to help someone else feel great too.

When the day has ended, dare to feel as you've done your best.

Dare to be the best you can –

At all times, Dare to be!"

NOTE TO SELF…

Doing the right thing can sometimes be hard, but when you do, the feeling it brings is indescribable.

Henry O from Plano

STEP TEN

Do the Right Thing (Make the Right Decision)

We may endure, accept and put up with many things in life. There are times when it is difficult to do the right thing, to make the right decision. Every day we are faced with making decisions. It is important that we make good choices and sound decisions. We must develop those common sense qualities that God has given each of us. Common sense can help us understand that we can find some success in our tragedies, in our failures and in our disappointments. It makes the pursuit of doing the right thing and making decisions without fear easier. Common Sense makes it possible to gain knowledge from every experience and apply that knowledge to our decision making.

What does doing the right thing mean to you?

1._____

_____

2._____

_____

3._____

_____

4._____

_____

5._____

_____

6._____

_____

The Secret To Success
... Unknown author

"Sir, what is the secret of your success?"
a reporter asked a bank president.

"Two words."

"And, sir, what are they?"

"Good Decisions."

"And how do you make good Decisions?"

"One word."

"And sir, what is that?"

"Experience."

"And how do you get Experience?"

"Two words."

"And, sir, what are they?"

"Bad Decisions."

Common Sense for Life/ Make the Right Decision
Common Sense makes it possible to gain knowledge from every experience and apply that knowledge to our decision making.

1. Pray before you make your decisions. Prayer keeps you closely connected to GOD.

   Call to me and I will answer you, and will tell you great and hidden things that you have not known. ...Jeremiah 33:3 ESV

2. Study the Word before you make major decisions. If the word says don't do it. Don't do it.

   If any of you lacks wisdom, let him ask God, who gives generously to all without reproach, and it will be given him. ...James 1:5 ESV

3. If you have doubts or you are not sure your decision is right. Don't do it.

   It is good not to eat meat or drink wine or do anything that causes your brother to stumble. ...Romans 14:21

4. Don't make a decision that doesn't feel good or have a good appearance.

   but test them all; hold on to what is good, reject every kind of evil. ...1 Thessalonians 5:21-22 (NIV)

5. Be obedient to GOD and let Him lead you in your decision making so that He might bless you. All blessing comes through obedience to GOD.

   I am setting before you today a blessing and a curse— the blessing if you obey the commands of the LORD your God that I am giving you today; ...Deuteronomy 11:26-27 (NIV)

6. When you have important decisions to make, always seek Godly counsel.

   Plans fail for lack of counsel, but with many advisers they succeed. ...Proverbs 15:22 (NIV)

7. Trust God and keep the faith in your decision making. He knows exactly what you need and when you need it.

   Trust in the Lord with all your heart, and do not lean on your own understanding. In all your ways acknowledge him, and he will make straight your paths. ...Proverbs 3:5-6 ESV

The Wisdom of Decision Making

1. "Where there is no decision there is no life."- JJ Dewey

2. "Choices are the hinges of destiny." – Pythagoras

3. "The risk of a wrong decision is preferable to the terror of indecision." – Maimonides

4. "Using the power of decision gives you the capacity to get past any excuse to change any and every part of your life in an instant." – Anthony Robbins

5. "Decision is a sharp knife that cuts clean and straight; indecision, a dull one that hacks and tears and leaves ragged edges behind it."- Gordon Graham

6. "Changing our decision sets up a bad habit. It reinforces decision-making as an expression of bewilderment and ignorance, instead of wisdom and freedom." – Sakyong Mipham

7. "The only real failure in life is not to be true to the best one knows." – Buddha

8. "The quality of decision is like the well-timed swoop of a falcon which enables it to strike and destroy its victim." – Sun Tzu

9. "Once you make a decision, the universe conspires to make it happen." – Ralph Waldo Emerson

The Importance of Decision Making

1. The decision you make today determines the fate of your tomorrow.

2. Don't be afraid to make the decisions.

3. Most people don't know what they don't know, but think they know ... as a result they remain ignorant.

4. Make your own decisions don't let others decide your life for you.

5. In order to do something you have never done, you must become someone you have never been.

6. You get in life what you are. (Les Brown)

7. The uncommitted life is not worth living. (Socrates)

8. Faith comes by hearing and hearing and hearing.

Appendix

About the Author

Henry O. Adkins is a State of Texas licensed Social Work Associate, a certified Life Coach and a member of the American Association of Christian Counselors (AACC). He is also Minister For Marriage and Family Enrichment at The Cedar Crest Church of Christ in Dallas, Texas.

Henry O. has had several successful careers. He spent over 20 years as a professional Jazz, Gospel and Blues Musician, performing with such greats as Freddie King, Lou Rawls, Roots First Edition, Dallas Gospel Fusion and Z.Z. Hill. He is also a watercolor artist specializing in rural and countryside landscapes.

He spent over 25 years as a government Administrator (10 years at the federal level and 15 years in city government). He spent 30 years as an adjunct professor of Political Science/Government at the undergraduate level and Political Science/Social Justice/Environmental Justice at the graduate level. Other College level positions included, Program Manager for Employment and Training (Richland College), Visiting Scholar (Mountain View College), Director of Community Services (Mountain View College) and Program Manager for Continuing Education (Cedar Valley College).

Henry O is the author of several books including the bestseller, "Life Lessons" Common Sense: Your Way To Success, Common Sense Parents, co-authored with his wife Sue, Common Sense Your Way Through College and "Common Sense Marriage". He has published numerous articles with such publications as the American Association of Christian Counselors, the American Society of Public Administration, University of Texas at Arlington Literary Journal, Dallas Baptist University Literary Review as well as many other periodicals and newspaper articles.

Suggested Reading

Five Keys To Sharing A Vision *by Robert E. Criner*
How To Keep Yourself Motivated *by Robert E. Criner*
The Sky's The Limit *by Dr. Wayne Dyer*
Don't Sweat The Small Stuff *by Richard Carlson, Ph.D.*
Chicken Soup For The Soul *by Jack Canfield and Mark V. Hansen*
Common Sense Parents *by Sue and Henry O. Adkins*
foreword by Robert E. Criner
How To Get Rich On Purpose *by DeWayne Owens*
The Positive Principle Today *by Norman Vincent Peale*
You Can Bounce Back *by Douglas McDuffie*
Turn Sets Into Greenbacks *by Willie Jolley*
A Setback Is A Setup For A Comeback *by Willie Jolley*
Common Sense Marriage *by Henry O. Adkins*
Think And Grow Rich *by Napoleon Hill*
The Power Of Positive Thinking *by Norman Vincent Peale*
Success Is In Our Race *by George Frasier*
Live Your Dreams *by Les Brown*
The Power of Purpose *by Les Brown*
Life Lessons/ Common Sense: Your Way To Success *by Henry O. Adkins*
foreword by Willie E. Jolley
The Power of Intention *by Wayne W. Dyer*
See You at the Top: 25th Anniversary Edition *by Zig Ziglar*
Embrace the Struggle: Living Life on Life's Terms
by Zig Ziglar and Julie Ziglar Norman

This workshop is based on Henry O. from Plano's book, Life Lessons/ "Common Sense: Your Way to Success". It is designed to help the participant pursue career opportunities successfully by applying a bit of book learning combined with a lot of Common Sense. This program shows how *Common sense will turn a breakdown into a breakthrough.*

To Order Multiple Copies of this workbook, please use this order form:

Name:_____

Address:_____

City: _____State /Prov: _____

Zip / Postal Code: _____Telephone(s): _____

_____copies @ $15.00 US / $18.00 Cdn: $_____

Shipping: ($5.00 first book - $1.50 each additional book) $_____

Texas residents add 8.25% tax $_____ Total amount enclosed

Mail to: Ten Steps… Cheudi Publishing, P.O. Box 940572-0572, Plano, Texas 75094

Cheudi Publishing
www.cheudi.com

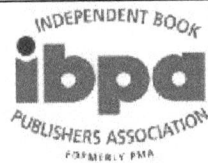

INDEPENDENT BOOK
ibpa
PUBLISHERS ASSOCIATION
FORMERLY PMA

Since 2003